TEEN LIFE™

FREQUENTLY ASKED QUESTIONS ABOUT

Overscheduling and Stress

Daniel E. Harmon

ROSEN
PUBLISHING®
New York

Published in 2010 by The Rosen Publishing Group, Inc.
29 East 21st Street, New York, NY 10010

Library of Congress Cataloging-in-Publication Data

Harmon, Daniel E.
Frequently asked questions about overscheduling and stress / Daniel E. Harmon.—1st ed.
    p. cm.—(FAQ: teen life)
Includes index.
ISBN 978-1-4358-3514-6 (library binding)
1. Stress management for teenagers. 2. Stress in adolescence. I. Title.
BF724.3.S86H37 2010
155.5'18—dc22

                                                    2009017825

Manufactured in Malaysia

CPSIA Compliance Information: Batch #TWW10YA: For Further Information contact Rosen Publishing, New York, New York at 1-800-237-9932

Contents

WHAT ARE OVERSCHEDULING AND STRESS?

"There aren't enough hours in a day."

Millions of Americans regularly repeat this saying, which seems so true: people have too many things to do and not enough time to do them.

In reality, people's bodies and minds are logically adapted to the daily cycle. They are geared to sleep approximately a third of the day. The big problem is that many people try to do too many activities during their waking hours. There are things they need to do each day and other things they want to do. Some people spend too much time with the things they and their friends want to do and then have to scramble to take care of the requirements. For others, schedule conflicts arise even though they carefully try to plan each day. Their problem is that they cram their days full, allowing no time for unexpected events. In either case, overscheduling is a common problem.

Overscheduling and other forms of stress can cause a young person to feel pulled in a hundred directions. The sense of hopelessness can lead to serious physical, mental, and emotional problems.

Overscheduling is just one cause of stress for young people as well as adults. Besides overscheduling, causes of stress include daily news (much of it negative), events that personally affect your life, and the expectations of friends and parents. Family feuds and feelings of guilt about misdoings or things you've neglected to do contribute. Causes also include demands and concerns that you place on yourself—efforts to get top grades in school, worry over your appearance or weight, the desire to be the best in athletics or cultural endeavors, and the need to prove that you are practically an adult.

Everyone experiences stress. Too much of it, though, can bring about serious long-term problems. The effects are worse on some people than others.

Dr. Hans Selye coined the term "stress" and discussed its impact on humans in his 1956 book, *The Stress of Life*. Stress is a state of frustration, weariness, anger, anxiety, and fear brought on by a variety of unpleasant events or situations. The word "stress" is a shortened form of "distress." It derives from a Latin word that suggests being "torn apart." Many Americans today truly feel "torn apart" by unhappy forces in their lives.

Stress Is a Natural Reaction

Stress is a chemical process. Kenneth R. Ginsburg and Martha M. Jablow, in "A Teen's Personalized Guide to Managing Stress," published by the American Academy of Pediatrics, describe stress as "the uncomfortable feeling you get when you're worried, scared, angry, frustrated, or overwhelmed. It is caused by emotions, but it affects your mood and body."

HelpGuide.org, an online resource, explains, "When you perceive a threat, your nervous system responds by releasing a flood of stress hormones, including adrenaline and cortisol. These hormones rouse the body for emergency action." The results? Your muscles tighten, your heart thumps loudly, and your breathing races. That's natural—and good. You are forced to evaluate the situation and decide whether "fight or flight" is your best response.

Adrenaline is the hormone that speeds the pulse and produces abnormally high energy. Another key stress hormone is

This is a microscopic image of cortisol, one of the main stress hormones. Interestingly, cortisol sometimes is prescribed by doctors to treat severe inflammation and other ailments.

cortisol. It sends more sugar into your bloodstream and controls how your brain applies it in response to stress. Cortisol affects a person's immune system, growth processes, reproductive system, and digestive system. The body's nervous system and hormones are your biological weapons for combating stress. In ordinary circumstances, they are enough.

Medical scientists point out that certain stressors, or stress causers, are good. Selye described "eustress" as positive stress. It alerts people to impending calamities, such as an automobile collision. It urges students to prepare for exams. The opposite of eustress, he wrote, is "distress," or negative stress. This is the mounting, ongoing kind of stress that can discourage a person and, if uncontrolled, can even ruin a life.

The Mayo Clinic, a medical treatment and study center based in Minnesota (with branches in Florida and Arizona), describes the two principal kinds of stress this way: "Acute"

Studying for a major exam can be stressful, but this is not necessarily a bad form of stress. Psychologists explain that stress is a natural part of life.

stress is what psychiatrists call "fight-or-flight" stress. It occurs when your body must instantly react to a threat or challenge. "The acute-stress response is immediate, it's intense, and in certain circumstances, it can be thrilling. Examples of stressors that may cause an acute-stress response are a job interview, a fender bender, or an exhilarating ski run," states the Mayo Clinic.

"Chronic" (negative) stress is far more serious. "The stressors that may lead to chronic stress are the nagging, day-to-day life situations that often seem unrelenting," the Mayo Clinic explains.

In 2007, the Foundation for Integrated Research in Mental Health reported that three out of five visits to doctors' offices result from stress. The American Psychological Association

(APA) in 2005 reported that almost two-thirds of Americans are attempting to reduce stress. The APA noted that stress has been linked to all six of the leading causes of death in the United States: heart disease, cancer, lung and liver diseases, accidents, and suicide. According to a survey by the Better Sleep Council, 65 percent of Americans lose sleep as a result of stress.

There is no formula for stress management because people are different. A heavy daily routine might cause severe stress for one fifteen year old. Another fifteen year old may have no problem with the same schedule and, in fact, may cheerfully thrive in the busy lifestyle. A person's overall disposition and attitude affect the ability to manage stress. Various things going on in the person's life—family problems, romantic relationships, etc.—also have an impact.

Stressful Schedules

The alarm clock sounds, or a rude shake and shout by a parent or sibling awakes you from your dream world. How will you spend your day? There are so many things you want to do—and all those activities you have to do get in the way. When you try to cram it all in, day after day, high stress can result.

Most months of the year, school is the main item on the schedules of most young people. Regular school hours occupy almost a third of the day, or roughly half of the waking hours. Homework may require several additional hours. Sports and other extracurricular activities can add several more hours. Many teenagers work part-time.

That leaves little family time. Meals are often wolfed down while on the run, in ten minutes or less. Many days, there is little or no time for relaxing in front of the television or going on the Internet, or for chatting with friends. For some adolescents, every day is packed with nonstop activities from when they rise in the morning until they collapse in bed at night.

In many families, parents contribute to the overscheduled lives of their children. Parents press children to excel and take advantage of every opportunity. In their classic study, *The Overscheduled Child: Avoiding the Hyper-Parenting Trap*, Dr. Alvin Rosenfeld and Nicole Wise say, "We may be busy already, but if our child has some particular talent or a hankering to try a new activity, and we can find a tiny window of time through which to squeeze it into our schedule, why not give it a go?"

Not everyone agrees that overscheduling is a harmful form of stress for children. Writing in *Time* magazine, John Cloud cites evidence that although children are "indisputably more scheduled now," it isn't necessarily a bad thing. Some research, he found, suggests that "most of the scheduling is beneficial: kids' well-being tends to improve when they participate in extracurriculars."

Human "Multitasking"

"No single event makes a life," say Rosenfeld and Wise. "It is the sum of all of them interacting with the temperament we brought with us into the world."

"Multitasking," a computing term, refers to a computer's ability to run several programs at the same time. You might have

By "multitasking," people can accomplish many things at once—for example, eating and listening to music while surfing the Internet. If people aren't careful, though, multitasking can contribute to stress.

your e-mail program, Web browser, calendar, word processor, and photo editor all open simultaneously. A click of the mouse or touch of the screen takes you instantly from one to another.

Some psychologists fear that multitasking has become a regular way of life for many Americans. People, especially young people, are constantly juggling many tasks at once: texting a message to one friend while talking to another on the home phone while eating spaghetti while watching television while reading (and supposedly absorbing) tomorrow's history assignment. If teenagers were robots, operating on computer programs and oiled regularly by their owners, they could probably accomplish more. But as humans, they have limitations and complex requirements (rest, recreation, discipline, relationships, emotional support, a sense of worth, and a set of goals, among many others). Too much multitasking, especially when combined with overscheduling, will eventually take its toll. They will begin to despair that they "don't have a life."

Myths and Facts

Myth **Having an overscheduled life comes from the high expectations that other people place on you.**

Fact: ➡ Overscheduling in young peoples' lives can come from many sources. It can result from the pressure that parents, friends, teachers, and the community put on teens to be competitive. Or it can come from teens' own high expectations for themselves and their drive to excel and overachieve.

Some of my friends swear that amphetamines and other stimulant drugs increase their energy and allow them to get more things done. Is there anything wrong with that?

Fact: ➡ Amphetamines are illegal unless prescribed by a doctor. They may cause or contribute to heart problems, anxiety attacks, exhaustion, violent behavior, and other physical and mental health dangers. Because stimulation is short-lived, many users require regular (and increasingly heavy) doses to produce continuing "benefits." Drug dependence can result.

If not relieved, stress can plunge you into deep depression.

Fact: ➡ The causes of clinical depression are not altogether clear and may include such factors as genetics. Stress certainly can worsen the symptoms. Studies have shown, for example, that simple actions like changes in a person's sleep-wake schedule can trigger an episode of depression. Doctors at the Mayo Clinic report that "environmental factors, such as stress, may play a role" in depression.

TWO

WHY CAN'T YOU HAVE A LIFE?

Young people face mounting time pressures. Sources include homework demands, which increase year by year, and pressure to maintain top grades if a student plans to go to college and perhaps earn a scholarship. Everyone enjoys recreational activities, and some—especially when lured by invitations from classmates and friends—spend too much time at play. Television and the Internet can be serious time stealers. Sports, music, dance, and other activities account for many after-school hours. A part-time job obviously adds to time stress.

Some people can juggle many obligations and activities and still "have a life." For others, daily demands are overwhelming—and personal problems present serious complications. The Web site HelpGuide.org states, "Beyond a certain point, stress stops being helpful and starts causing major damage to your health, your mood, your productivity, your relationships, and your quality of life."

Never a Dull Moment

School is a requirement. How a teen spends after-school hours is an issue in scheduling and stress management.

Young people who participate in school sports and other after-school activities face a formidable scheduling challenge. Football, baseball, hockey, track, cross-country, basketball, volleyball, golf, wrestling, and other sports call for regular

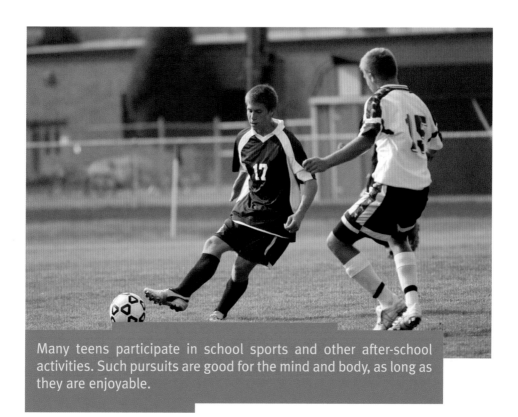

Many teens participate in school sports and other after-school activities. Such pursuits are good for the mind and body, as long as they are enjoyable.

practices lasting two to three hours—sometimes longer—after school. Games and matches may last well into the evening, once or twice per week. When events occur in distant towns, travel time further affects players' personal schedules. Some competitions take place on Saturdays; including drive time, they can occupy the whole day.

Teenage athletes involved in just one sport get at least half the year off (although they're expected to keep themselves in shape year-round). Many, though, compete in two or three sports. This involvement keeps them committed to regular practices throughout the school year.

Some sports are not seasonal. It is not uncommon for top swimmers to be in the pool early each morning and again in the afternoon—ten or eleven months per year, in many cases. Some young hockey players practice five or six days each week and compete year-round.

School band and orchestra members typically rehearse during school periods, but they are expected to regularly practice at home. Students who take private lessons in music, gymnastics, dance, horseback riding, karate, or another activity must commit to a weekly visit with the instructor (including drive time), plus practice time at home. Other school activities—involvement with the school newspaper, yearbook, or various clubs—may require extra time to attend meetings and perform after-school tasks.

Child psychiatrists note that private tutoring is a fast-growing activity. Tutoring is recommended for children who really need it, they agree—but perhaps not for those whose parents are demanding more A's and fewer B's on the report card. In many

A student receives standard tutoring in a library program. Some parents enroll their children for special tutoring in advanced subjects—which can impose a scheduling burden.

cases, parents have their children tutored in subjects at advanced grade levels.

Some children are driven 40 or 50 miles (about 64 to 81 kilometers) round-trip to cultural lessons or tutoring. The child might spend the drive time reading and studying—but not so in the case of teenagers who drive themselves. Private lessons may continue year-round.

A few young people have special (not required) activities scheduled seven days each week. They enjoy a rich variety of rewarding experiences, developing their talents and interests in many directions. When stress begins to squeeze a life, though, the enjoyment diminishes. Activities that once were fun become obligations.

Structured Lives

It has been noted that children today often don't do things "just for fun" like their parents and grandparents did. They don't go into the yard as much to simply throw a football or baseball. They have to join a league and participate "officially"—and feel pressured to excel and perhaps earn a high school letter and even a college scholarship.

Dr. Sid Kirchheimer, writing at MedicineNet.com, observes that "in the past 20 years, the number of children who partici-pate in organized youth sports has doubled—yet teens who try out for their high school's sports team have reached an all-time low." Translation: By about age thirteen, many young people have had enough of the regular after-school practices and the screaming at games. It isn't fun anymore.

Kirchheimer continues, "There's no argument that these [preteen] activities are helpful. Valuable life lessons and plenty of fun result from learning 'Chopsticks,' building Pinewood Derby racers, and playing team sports. The concern is that young chil-dren may be getting too much of a good thing—especially before they should."

Most medical professionals agree that no one pattern of activ-ity is appropriate for all young people. Child development authority Dr. David Elkind, author of *The Unhurried Child*, sug-gests general weekly limitations. He advises at MedicineNet.com that for elementary school students, "there should be no more than three activities—one sport, one social activity like Scouts, and one artistic endeavor like music lessons or art class. And they should only go for an hour or so to each one each week. It's really inappropriate for elementary school children to go to daily practices."

Parental Pressure

Parents naturally want their children to succeed. To ensure that, many of them try to instill ambition and a constant sense of drive. Children who are gifted in particular areas may feel pressured by their parents to apply enormous amounts of time and rise to the very top in performance and competition. Some parents impose unending structure in almost every area of their children's routines, believing that this is the way for their children to get the most out of life.

Child psychiatrist Alvin Rosenfeld, writing with coauthor Nicole Wise in *The Overscheduled Child*, warns, "Children whose every moment is scheduled and structured because their parents want them to have the benefit of everything the world has to offer may have difficulty learning how to be alone, and at peace, with themselves." He adds, "We need to remember whose life it is after all and to let our children have the freedom they need to live their own and to learn from it."

This regimented approach to parenting is not surprising. Rosenfeld and Wise, both parents, point out that "every time we pick up the paper, turn on the news, or try to lose ourselves in the pages of a magazine, someone else is adding something new

Young people should discuss scheduling issues with their parents. Sometimes, parents pressure their children to be more active; other times, young people pressure themselves.

to the list of things we are supposed to be doing for our children to make sure they turn out right."

Parental pressure takes other forms. A mother who lectures at a university may find it unthinkable that her daughter makes less than A's in school. A father who played college football may press his son to shine on the high school field and win an athletic scholarship. A parent who is a talented musician may insist that a child take lessons and master the same instrument. If no one in a parent's family ever attended college, the parent may lean heavily on a child to make top grades and pursue a college degree.

Some children reject such expectations, but many try hard—and spend countless hours—trying to fulfill them. As Rosenfeld and Wise observe, "Children feel a deep inner need to prove their value to their parents."

It is one thing for a parent to encourage a child, another to exert undue pressure. Kirchheimer, writing at MedicineNet.com, reports, "Many kids are more frenzied than ever because of overzealous parents who think the more activities a child does, the greater the likelihood of creating a trophy child: Scouts. Little League. Music lessons. Dance recitals. It's not uncommon to see a well-marked kitchen calendar of scheduled events that is just as crammed as many CEOs'."

Carleton Kendrick, a family therapist, author, and lecturer, says, "The phenomenon of parents overscheduling their kids' lives and stealing their childhood is all too real. Many parents fill up their kids' lives with one 'enrichment activity' after another, starting in the early preschool years, all in an effort to help them 'get a leg up' so that they will eventually gain admittance to a top-ranked college."

Kendrick urges that children need free time—"unstructured time, time to dream, time to discover—and yes, to even become a little bored once in a while."

Self-Pressure

On the other hand, some children exert too much pressure on themselves to succeed. Do you have friends who agonize if they can't be the best at something? Some children set their

Some children are eager to participate in multiple activities, and they push themselves to be "the best" at everything. Yet over time, these activities and expectations can produce tension.

own self-expectations too high. Their parents may assure and reassure them that a perfect report card (although wonderful) is not required. Still, the child is devastated by those two B's among the A's.

Other young people are overly eager to do everything that there is to do. They feel a need to sign up for every sport and cultural activity that they possibly can. Perhaps you have friends who are frantically stressed for that reason. After they have enrolled in every activity that interests them, they don't seem to understand why pressure begins to quickly build and their lives become very unhappy. But it's obvious to you. Maybe they could benefit from your casual, friendly opinion.

Behavioral specialists observe that parents tend to avoid restraining their ambitious children who overschedule themselves. Even if they begin to notice signs of stress, they are reluctant to tell their child, "You really need to cut out some of your activities, or you'll go crazy." It might take a caring friend to get the message across.

Temptations, Temptations

Meanwhile, many young people simply squander so much time that even light schedules become crises. There is television, the cell phone, the iPod, the Internet, and the computer with all the latest action games. There are the parties and outings with friends to dinner, concerts, and movies.

Social networking has developed into a growing time consumer in recent years, especially among young people. With Facebook, YouTube, Twitter, and other networks, people keep in steady contact with friends old and new. Other forms of constant interaction with friends and family include texting and instant messaging, not to mention "old-fashioned" e-mail.

Personal withdrawal can be another time user. Some people spend hours daydreaming. Psychiatrists say that personal downtime is very important—to a certain extent. People need to spend time by themselves planning, sorting through problems, thinking about friends and relationships, and yes, daydreaming. Frequent and prolonged withdrawal can be a sign of depression or anxiety, though. And when it contributes to a buildup of tasks left undone, it adds to stress.

These various forms of pressure—school, peer expectations, parental structure, self-pressure, and excessive loafing—can be stressors if they are not managed. Even an enjoyable activity can become a stressor if you know that you need to be doing something else during that time.

three

WHEN DO OVERSCHEDULING AND STRESS BEGIN TO AFFECT YOU?

Everyone has encountered stress. The Nemours Foundation's TeensHealth Web site, KidsHealth.org, explains there is "good stress and bad stress." While driving, for instance, hitting the brakes to avoid a wreck obviously is a positive stress reaction. "The stress response . . . can also be activated in a milder form at a time when the pressure's on but there's no actual danger—like stepping up to take the foul shot that could win the game, getting ready to go to a big dance, or sitting down for a final exam."

Too many daily, long-term obligations, on the other hand, are bad stress. A few minutes itemizing how you spend your time any given day, from waking up in the morning to going to bed at night, can alert you to the fact that you have an overscheduling problem. If you

Headaches can be a physical symptom of stress. So can stomachaches, twitching and trembling, and tense muscles. The symptoms can worsen over time.

have to be at a rehearsal or other event at 6:30 AM and other regular activities involve you from then until after dark—leaving you scant time for homework or relaxation with family and friends—you are clearly overextended. For a while, you can survive, gritting your teeth and trudging through the daily grind. Eventually, the stress will tell.

According to HelpGuide.org, "Long-term exposure to stress can lead to serious health problems. Chronic stress disrupts nearly every system in your body. It can raise blood pressure, suppress the immune system, increase the risk of heart attack and stroke, contribute to infertility, and speed up the aging process. Long-term stress can even rewire the brain, leaving you more vulnerable to anxiety and depression."

General symptoms of overscheduling and stress include exhaustion, sleeplessness, irritability (bad temper), sadness, forgetfulness, a dysfunctional plodding through daily routines, constant worrying, and anxiety. Physical symptoms can include headaches and stomachaches, back pain, nausea and diarrhea, muscle tension, twitching, trembling, dizziness, and sweating.

Warning Signs

Symptoms of stress take four forms: physical, mental, emotional, and social. Physical symptoms may include tiredness and headaches. Mental symptoms may include difficulty focusing on tasks and remembering things. Emotional symptoms are typically anxiety, sadness, and feelings of hopelessness. There are also what psychologists call "social symptoms," such as bitterness and anger toward people you know—sometimes including your friends—or withdrawal.

HelpGuide.org states, "The most dangerous thing about stress is how easily it can creep up on you. You get used to it. It starts to feel familiar—even normal. You don't notice how much it's affecting you, even as it takes a heavy toll."

A Mayo Clinic newsletter confirms this perception: "Stress symptoms may be affecting your health, even though you might not realize it. You may think illness is to blame for that nagging headache, your forgetfulness or your decreased productivity at work. But sometimes stress is to blame."

To paraphrase a popular comedian, you know you have an overscheduled life when:

- You lie awake at night wondering how you can possibly do everything that you're supposed to do tomorrow.

- You worry about almost everything.
- You have trouble keeping appointments.
- You feel too guilty to turn down an invitation to play tennis, even though you're under pressure to complete a science project.
- Your grades in school nudge downward.
- You lash out impatiently—even at people you love—when you feel time obligations pressing in.
- You still feel exhausted after a normal night's sleep.
- You feel overwhelmed with hopelessness.
- You begin eating between meals, sometimes when you aren't even hungry.
- You consider indulging in risky substances to improve your mental state.
- You have headaches, upset stomach, and other physical ailments for no apparent reason.
- Your days are filled with things to do, often taking you in many directions at once. But inside, you feel unfulfilled.
- You find yourself zoning out with television.
- You've flirted with thoughts of "ending it all."

Heed the signals.

Are You or a Friend at Particular Risk?

The Mayo Clinic reports that some individuals are more at risk for stress than others. Reasons can include their personal temperaments and characteristics. Overscheduling naturally creates

Many young people enjoy school sports, teamwork, and competition. Their motivations may be sound, but the time commitments are burdensome, especially for multisport athletes.

problems for those who are most susceptible. "Persistent or chronic stress has the potential to put vulnerable individuals at a substantially increased risk of depression, anxiety, and many other emotional difficulties."

Many child psychiatrists and counselors worry that the lives of most children, no matter how strong or vulnerable a young person might be, are more dangerously overscheduled today than in past generations. Kendrick says, "Professionally, I have seen more and more young children experiencing stress-related psychosomatic symptoms—headaches, stomach-aches, insomnia, anxiety attacks—caused by pressure and overscheduling."

Sports and other competitive activities may call for extra stress-handling abilities. Competition can be good for the body and the mind. It can propel people to great heights. It obviously requires dedication and no small effort. If you push yourself (or are pushed by parents, coaches, or other competitors) too hard, however, you may find that winning is not worth the stress. Alvin Rosenfeld and Nicole Wise note, "In recent years, Little League has become as competitive as the Majors."

Sleep Loss and Stress: A Brutal Cycle

Beginning in high school—earlier, in some cases—teenagers significantly alter their sleep regimens, especially on weekends, when they enjoy outings with friends. They no longer go to sleep at eleven o'clock at night and rise at six-thirty in the morning. Instead, many teens go out at eleven on Fridays and Saturdays, return home at perhaps four in the morning, and sleep until noon or later the next day.

This change in the sleep-wake pattern raises several issues with children and their parents. Among others, it creates a scheduling dilemma. Suppose you have several exciting activities planned for Saturday. If you aren't out of bed and ready to begin any of them until the afternoon, how can you expect to complete more than one or two before you begin your Saturday nightlife? If this cycle repeats on Saturday night and carries over to Sunday afternoon and evening (and if you have school assignments due Monday morning), you definitely have a weekend scheduling problem.

Teens, many counselors think, generally do not get enough sleep. Some say high school is scheduled "too early." That is, adolescents, by nature, typically cannot get to sleep before 11:00 PM—and they need to rise for school by 6:00 AM.

The simple practice of overscheduling cuts into the number of hours a person has available for sleep. Other forms of stress also impair sleep. Consequences of inadequate sleep can include irritability and anger during the day, difficulty concentrating and remembering, poor decision making, awkwardness, dangerous driving, a weakened frame of mind that makes it harder to cope with stress, and reduced productivity. According to the ISYT.com (It's Stealing Your Time) Web project, "Studies have shown that people who sleep less than six hours a night are at a higher risk of motor vehicle crashes."

There are more long-term risks, too. Sleep deprivation results in increased levels of cortisol, the stress hormone. Over time, excessive cortisol levels can weaken immunity. Inadequate sleep

Obesity often results from a combination of causes, including unhealthy eating habits in response to stress. Sleep deprivation, another symptom of stress, also can contribute to weight gain.

can also slow down the body's production of glucose. The result is weight gain.

It is vital for people to get what the Better Sleep Council calls "healthy, restorative sleep." The council offers suggestions for improving your sleep time. Among them are the following:

- Give sleep a high priority in your schedule.
- Develop a relaxing bedtime routine (lowered lights, soft music, a hot bath, passive reading—not tense dramas or horror).
- Keep computers and even TV sets out of the bedroom.
- Don't smoke or consume caffeinated drinks near bedtime. Don't eat within two or three hours of going to bed.
- Make sure you have a comfortable, supportive mattress and pillows. (The council recommends that pillows be replaced annually.)

Some doctors advise against napping during the day because it will disturb your regular nighttime sleep pattern. Some believe it is wise to let adolescents sleep a few hours later on weekend mornings. Others, though, recommend regular bedtimes and wake-up times, seven days a week. This discipline, they say, establishes an internal sleep-wake cycle (you may not even need an alarm clock) and results in better-quality sleep. Doctors suggest that a lower than normal nighttime room temperature enhances sleep.

How many hours of sleep do people need? Small children need up to ten hours each night. Typical adults need roughly eight hours, according to most studies. For many years, scientists believed teenagers needed about as much sleep as adults. Some suggested they could get by with less. More recent research indicates that adolescents may need as much as nine-and-a-half hours of sleep to function at their best.

Remember that sleep problems contribute to stress and vice-versa. People who are lacking enough sleep tend to suffer from deepened stress and are unable to handle it well. Unresolved stresses of the day contribute to worried tossing and turning at night. If not corrected, erratic (inconsistent) scheduling and sleep patterns can contribute to severe stress with long-term consequences.

four

WHAT ARE THE LONG-TERM EFFECTS?

When overscheduling and other problems combine to create severe stress, results can be dangerous and long lasting. According to the Mayo Clinic, "The long-term activation of the stress-response system—and the subsequent overexposure to cortisol and other stress hormones—can disrupt almost all your body's processes." The clinic points out that chronic stress (prolonged exposure to pressures) is subtler than acute stress (sudden crises or challenges). Its effects can be complicated.

The long-term effects of stress might range from major to minor. Stress can contribute significantly to terminal diseases. People with chronic medical conditions may experience a flare-up of their illness during times of great stress. Stress can contribute to lesser ailments, such as eczema and other skin conditions.

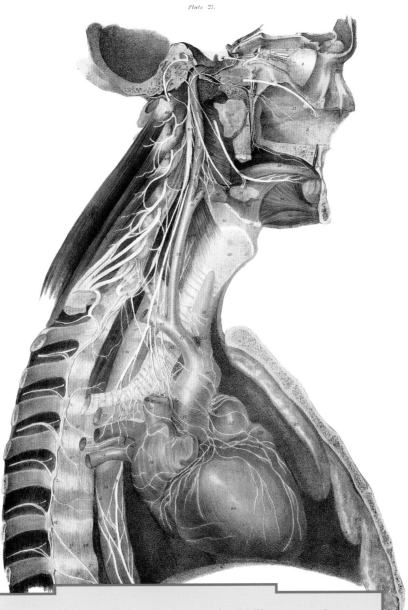

Plate 27.

This cutaway view of the upper human body illustrates the sympathetic nervous system (SNS), which affects major organs and physical processes. The SNS uses hormones to handle stress.

That's because during periods of stress, certain hormones limit blood flow to the skin.

The Franklin Institute, which provides online resources on science and health topics, has studied the effects of stress on the brain. It reports that stress particularly affects a person's ability to learn and remember things. "As science gains greater insight into the consequences of stress on the brain, the picture that emerges is not a pretty one. A chronic overreaction to stress overloads the brain with powerful hormones that are intended only for short-term duty in emergency situations. Their cumulative [combined] effect damages and kills brain cells."

Humans have what doctors refer to as a "sympathetic nervous system" (SNS) and a "parasympathetic nervous system" (PNS). These processes use certain hormones to cope with stress and other hormones to relax. The SNS triggers our natural "fight-or-flight" reaction to a stressor. When the crisis passes, the PNS returns us to normal.

The SNS and PNS carry on what the Franklin Institute likens to a tug-of-war inside our bodies. "The trouble is that some stress hormones don't know when to quit pulling. They remain active in the brain for too long—injuring and even killing cells." Doctors warn that when a person's nervous system is in constant fight-or-flight mode, serious health issues can result.

Much depends on the type of stress that a person experiences. To a moderate extent, scheduling demands can healthily serve to keep a person busy and productive. Deadlines and memory challenges, according to some research, can aid the human immune system. Violent stress, however, can hamper immunity.

And any type of stress, if overwhelming and extended, can be harmful.

Overeating and Substance Abuse

People innocently call it "comfort food": irregular and often unhealthy snacks and meals to relieve stress. Many teenagers who live with relentless scheduling pressure and other forms of stress turn to food as a momentary escape. (The wise ones instead resort to an exercise break.) The most tempting comfort food is rich in calories, trans fats, and other problematic ingredients.

Unhealthy eating is a worsening trend. Studies show that more than 30 percent of American teenagers and preteens are either overweight or at risk with their weight—more than three times the percentage of young people who had that problem in the 1970s. Many are obese.

This issue feeds on itself when coupled with stress. That is, an unhealthy body size increases the emotional stress on an individual who is already staggering beneath a schedule over-load. Meanwhile, excess weight causes physical ailments, even among teenagers. It strains joints, causes labored breathing, and raises blood pressure. It can literally slow you down, making it more difficult for you to meet obligations.

Weight problems at an early age can become a lifetime pat-tern if they're not reversed. The long-term effects are frightening. Obesity—or even moderate excess weight, for some people—contributes to heart and circulatory diseases, diabetes, breathing disorders, osteoarthritis and hip/knee malfunctions, liver disease, and sociopsychological problems.

All too often, the "comfort food" people reach for when they're under pressure is fatty and caloric. Unhealthy eating habits cause weight problems—which in turn contribute to stress.

Another dangerous escape from overscheduling is substance abuse. Many young users of hallucinogens, for example, say they turn to them to dodge stress and forget unhappiness. Some teenagers illegally drink alcoholic beverages for the same reason. Dr. David Walsh, a psychologist, cites statistics that suggest almost a third of high school seniors can be categorized as "heavy drinkers." So can 14 percent of eighth graders. "Heavy drinking," according to one study, means that at some point during the past two weeks, the person has had at least five drinks at one event.

Consuming drugs and alcohol might make people briefly forget their problems. But when users come to their senses, they realize they've lost valuable time. They find that their to-do lists have grown from critical to crisis status. In the meantime, they've injured their bodies. Walsh explains that the use of tobacco, alcohol, and other substances destroys brain cells. Brain cells can eventually be restored, but substance abuse can cause other damage. Especially in young people, it interferes with the chemicals that the brain uses to send messages from one part of the body to another. These chemicals are called neurotransmitters. Disrupting the function of neurotransmitters can impair people's—especially young people's—ability to learn new ideas and store information. Research indicates that heavy drinkers may have their normal memory capability damaged by as much as 10 percent, Walsh says. Even if a teenager stops using harmful substances, the learning and memory problems that result can last into young adulthood. He adds, "The earlier a youngster starts to drink, the higher the probability that he or she will have alcohol problems or alcoholism as an adult."

Nicotine from cigarettes also affects the brain's neurotransmitters. In studies, it has repeatedly been linked to cancer, heart disease, and other major illnesses. Research has made it clear that people who start smoking as adolescents are more likely to become addicted than those who start later in life. Psychologists refer to nicotine as a "gateway drug," a simple entry point for teenagers into widespread drug experimentation.

As with overeating, substance abuse during the early years can carry into adulthood. Many abused substances are addictive. All types of abused substances—food, alcohol, nicotine, and other

Active people should be careful about what they drink to quench their thirst or generate a burst of energy. Many soft drinks and energy drinks contain high levels of caffeine.

drugs—can create long-term and even permanent injuries to the body and mind.

A seemingly more innocent form of substance abuse is the consumption of caffeine. Caffeinated coffee has been considered a pick-me-up for hundreds of years. But caffeine can cause unhealthy complications, such as sleeplessness and nervous tension.

Popular among today's teenagers and adults are new sources of caffeine: "energy drinks" like Adrenaline Rush, Red Bull, and Venom. Many energy drinks contain heavy percentages of caffeine, ginseng, guarana, and/or other stimulants. Some contain as much caffeine as a cup of caffeinated coffee. Many soft drinks also contain caffeine, although not nearly as much as energy drinks. Energy drinks appeal to overscheduled young people who hope that these jolts of vigor will help them accomplish more in their allotted time. But researchers at Brown University warn that energy drinks "should be treated carefully."

In the short term, too much caffeine can increase blood pressure and prevent sleep. Long-term effects are being studied. Some scientists suspect that caffeine contributes to cancer and birth defects.

Adults actually encourage teenagers' use of certain unnatural substances. Some parents obtain prescription medicines like Ritalin, a mental stimulant, for their children to take before undergoing major exams and the SAT. Numerous teen athletes have taken steroids to increase their muscle tissue. Although it may have no serious side effects, any reliance on medicine to perform normal tasks is unwise.

Break Away from Bad Patterns

Rather than resort to drugs and other substances, which often come with perilous risks and frequently lead to long-term problems, teenagers should simply learn how to manage their time and stress. No chemical substance can permanently solve their pressure and time problems. It will only lead them farther down a risky path—possibly a course of dependency.

Poor scheduling skills in youth tend to carry into adulthood. There, the pressure will intensify. It can result in burnout, a negative outlook, and more subtle problems.

Ten Great Questions to Ask a Counselor

1 What are effective ways to better manage stress?

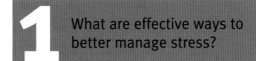

2 What changes in my diet can I make to improve my energy level and emotional ability to handle stress?

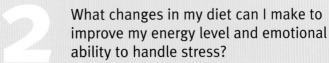

3 Would regular consumption of sports drinks ("energy drinks") and health foods help me accomplish more?

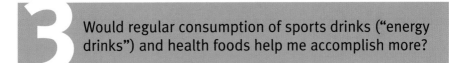

4 To me, Facebook and other forms of computer networking with my friends are an important way to relax. But I admit I waste a lot of time that way. How can I control my use of these Internet tools?

5 Do you recommend that I cut out some of my after-school activities? What should be my limit?

6 Assuming I need to eliminate activities, how should I prioritize my schedule?

7 With my present schedule, I know I don't have time for a part-time job, but my family and I need extra income. What should I do?

8 How can I tell my best friends, without offending them, to leave me alone because I need to study or get some sleep?

9 A friend's daily and weekly schedules are almost identical to mine, but she doesn't seem nearly as stressed as me. Why is that?

10 What books would you suggest young people read about managing schedules and stress?

five

HOW CAN YOU CONTROL STRESS?

How can you and your friends control your schedules and reduce stress? The solution, in short, is "Learn to manage it." HelpGuide's definition is as follows: "Stress management involves changing the stressful situation when you can, changing your reaction when you can't, taking care of yourself, and making time for rest and relaxation."

TeensHealth points out that stress management should be something you work at constantly, even when you're not feeling overscheduled or otherwise stressed. "Knowing how to 'de-stress' and doing it when things are relatively calm can help you get through challenging circumstances that may arise."

Countless self-help books on stress and schedule management have been published. And an Internet search on those and related terms will lead to thousands of

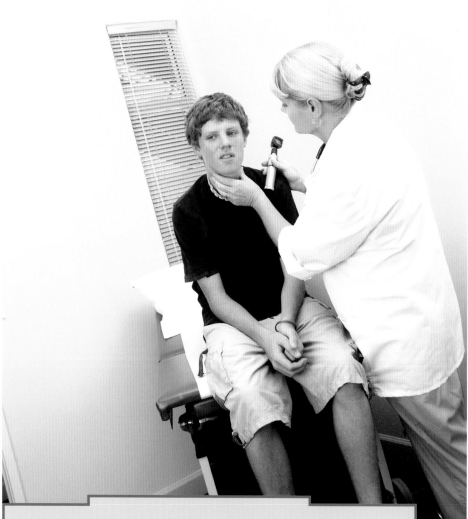

Regular medical checkups are advisable even for healthy young people. If you are experiencing serious stress symptoms, a consultation with a therapist or doctor is especially important.

Web resources published by reputable organizations, counselors, and authors.

The Mayo Clinic explains, "Many factors contribute to maintaining good mental health, including getting enough sleep, eating sensibly, exercising appropriately, avoiding use of harmful substances such as alcohol, and effectively managing stress. If you have chronic stress, consult a doctor or therapist to discuss ways to minimize stress and its negative impact on your physical and emotional health. He or she may recommend relaxation exercises, such as deep breathing or visualization, soothing activities, such as yoga or massage, or professional therapy."

Tips to Avoid Maxing Out and Burning Out

Health sources suggest numerous ways to control overscheduling and manage stress. They include the following:

- Identify your specific scheduling problems—items cluttering your schedule that might be eliminated.
- Perform your "must-do" tasks first. After they're put aside, your "fun" activities will be much more enjoyable.
- Do not accept an invitation to do anything, whether it's going out for ice cream with friends or joining a band, without considering the time commitment it will require. Consider how you will spend your time each day. Learn to say no to friends and others whose demands on your time would add to your stress.

One recommended stress reliever is simply to slow down and enjoy life. Leisure time with family and friends, or alone, can refresh your mindset.

- Slow down. Enjoy whatever it is you're doing at the moment without thinking about what you'll be doing the next moment. When talking to friends or relatives, pay full attention to what they're saying—don't worry about coming up with a clever reply.
- Spend quality time with family members and friends.
- Spend a little time each day being unproductive. Trying to be relentlessly productive is a ticket to burnout.
- Periodically block out an entire day on your calendar for plain enjoyment, with no scheduled events. In other

words, take the day off. Have fun! Recreation is as important as achievement.

- When an activity that was once fun turns into an obligation, give it up.

Ginsburg and Jablow, in "A Teen's Personalized Guide to Managing Stress," suggest two simple ideas for managing a heavy workload:

1. "Break work into small pieces. Then just do one small piece at a time, rather than look at the whole huge mess. As you finish each piece, the work becomes less overwhelming.
2. "Make lists of what you need to do. This will help you sleep because your head won't spin with worry about whether you can do everything. At the end of the day, you will have less to worry about as you check off the things you have finished. You will look at the same huge amount of homework and say to yourself, 'I can do this!'"

An interesting experiment is to turn off the television, computer, cell phone, iPod, and every other gadget you own for two days. You will probably feel horribly disconnected at first, but observe what eventually happens to your stress level during that downtime.

What's Most Important?

Decide your priorities in life. If you have a hard time sorting them out, get a parent or counselor to discuss them with you. As

Careful calendar planning is essential to avoiding an overscheduled life. It's helpful from time to time to review previous months' schedules to see how you've been spending your time.

you plan your schedule, start with the basic things that need to be done. Proceed with the things that are less important to you, in descending order. Are you passionate about some of the items that clutter your schedule? Are you uninterested in others, doing them only because friends or parents want you to be involved? If you feel overscheduled, start cutting activities from the bottom of your list, or give those things less time.

Young people who spend many hours every week striving to excel at one endeavor should count the costs and weigh the sacrifices. Earning the next belt in karate is great, and it certainly enhances your self-confidence. But years from now, when you may no longer be interested in karate at all, will you look back and wish you'd spent a lot of those hours doing different things? Bear in mind that you can devote your lifetime to becoming the best at something and still be left disappointed. When you think you have climbed the highest mountain, you notice a slightly taller peak not far away. Think about all the other interesting things in life that you could be doing instead of clambering for a championship.

In all competitions, there are many more losers than winners. The most important question is: Are you enjoying yourself?

Become Methodical

Handle tasks as they arise. (Remember the old adage: "Don't put off until tomorrow what you can do today.") Procrastination leads to a buildup of pressure. Take action.

Employ your time carefully. When doing homework, make every minute count. Don't let yourself become distracted.

Psychiatrists note that a useful technique for schedule management is to start by taking care of a small, easy obligation. This will give you feelings of control and confidence as you move on to larger items. It will demonstrate that if you apply yourself, you can really conquer your time monster.

Poor nutrition can both contribute to stress and result from it; good nutrition is a vital weapon for combating stress. Fruits and vegetables are staples of a wise diet.

Set goals for each day, and track your progress toward meeting them. Even if you know by heart what's on your agenda for the day, write down your schedule. Examine it from time to time, and consider if you might enjoy life more by losing some of those commitments.

Take Care of Your Mind

Psychiatrists know of many ways a person can manage stress. One way is learning to relax. For many people, yoga, tai chi, and other methods of relaxation are beneficial.

Train yourself to see the bright side of things. A positive, optimistic attitude is an important tool for stress management.

Exercise, rest, read, and communicate leisurely with friends and family. Many teenagers spend practically no time with the people they live with. That can be fairly simple to remedy. Rosenfeld and Wise, in *The Overscheduled Child*, observe, "Some very close families only eat dinner together on weekends and special occasions. But they find other ways and times to connect—at breakfast, after school, on weekends."

Good nutrition is important for both the body and mind. Eat regular, balanced meals. Occasional snacking is OK, nutritionists say, but be mindful of the unhealthiness of fatty foods and caffeinated drinks. The better your health, the better you can handle stress.

If you feel parental pressure to excel in school or participate in an activity that you think is unnecessary, sit down and discuss it with your parents. If a parent doesn't seem to understand, talk

There is a time for everything. Relaxing with your favorite music can be an excellent stress reliever—but too much leisure can leave important tasks undone, creating more stress.

to a school counselor about your problem. If necessary, get professional counseling to help you cope with stress.

Friends Don't Let Friends Waste Time

Observe symptoms of overscheduling and stress in your friends. Perhaps you can help them deal with the problem.

Above all, respect their time. Learn to recognize when you are intruding, even in fun and friendly ways. Friendship time is certainly important, but there is a big distinction between meaningful communication and idling. A quarter of an hour spent on the phone, instant messaging, or on Facebook's Wall-to-Wall feature may be delightful, compassionate, and relaxing for you both. But it might also distract your friend from completing a difficult science paper that's due tomorrow. Know when to stay away.

Meanwhile, don't let your friends violate your time. If you pay attention, you may notice that the friends who most frequently demand your time are the ones who have few time commitments themselves. They seem to figure that since they have little to do, you do, too.

Expect Stress—But Learn to Manage It

Melinda Smith and Ellen Jaffe, writing online in HelpGuide.org, observe, "Modern life is full of hassles, deadlines, frustrations, and demands. For many people, stress is so commonplace that it has become a way of life. Stress isn't always bad. In small doses, it can help you perform under pressure and motivate you to do your best. But when you're constantly running in emergency mode, your mind and body pay the price."

All professional counselors advise that people need time just for themselves, time to do those things that matter to them personally—and time to do nothing at all, if they choose. In order to create personal time, individuals have to say no to other people and never-ending time demands.

Learn to prioritize your time. There are things you must do, things you should do, things you'd like to do, and things other people pressure you to do. You can't do them all. What are the things that matter most to you? What are the things that, when you really think about them, devour much of your time but matter hardly at all? Commit to the first group. Say no to the rest.

chronic Having a particular long-term illness or condition.

dysfunctional Characterized by an inability to function emotionally or as a social unit; relating badly.

eczema A disease notable for skin inflammation.

extracurricular After-class involvement in school-related activities, including sports and clubs.

genetics Hereditary factors that affect a person's behavior and health.

glucose A form of sugar typically produced from cornstarch.

hallucinogen A chemical substance that causes a person to have an unreal, dreamlike experience.

immune system The body's chemical response processes that go into action when a germ or alien substance attacks the body.

neurotransmitter A chemical that the brain uses to carry instructions from one part of the body to another.

obese Extremely, dangerously overweight.

osteoarthritis A disease caused by constant heavy stress on the joints.

persistent Unrelenting; continuing despite treatment.

psychosomatic Relating to perceived physical symptoms brought about by mental factors, such as stress; involving both the mind and body.

social networking Connecting with friends, relatives, and acquaintances—and with their friends, relatives, and acquaintances—by using an Internet platform like Facebook or Twitter.

steroid A type of hormone that can affect the body in various ways, such as by contributing to the growth of muscle tissue.

stimulant A substance taken to promote increased physical activity or mental alertness.

stressor An event or situation that creates stress.

tai chi An ancient Chinese system for relaxation that combines exercise with meditation.

terminal Resulting in death; often refers to diseases like incurable cancer and certain heart conditions.

trans fat A type of fat containing unsaturated fatty acids; it contributes to high cholesterol levels.

vulnerable Physically or psychologically weak; unable to resist.

yoga An ancient Hindu method of controlling the mind and body, often practiced to relieve stress.

America on the Move Foundation
44 School Street, Suite 325
Boston, MA 02108
(800) 807-0077
Web site: http://www.americaonthemove.org
   The America on the Move Foundation promotes active
   living and healthy eating habits.

American Academy of Pediatrics
141 Northwest Point Boulevard
Elk Grove Village, IL 60007
(847) 434-4000
Web site: http://www.aap.org
   The American Academy of Pediatrics's Web site
   includes information on stress management for teens
   and parents.

American Institute of Stress
124 Park Avenue
Yonkers, NY 10703
(914) 963-1200
Web site: http://www.stress.org
   This nonprofit organization was established to serve as a
   clearinghouse of information on stress-related topics.

Better Sleep Council
501 Wythe Street
Alexandria, VA 22314-1917
Web site: http://www.bettersleep.org
   This nonprofit organization is "devoted to educating the
   public about the importance of sleep to good health and
   quality of life, and about the value of the sleep system
   and sleep environment in pursuit of a good night's sleep."

Canada's Physical Activity Guides for Children and Youth
Public Health Agency of Canada
Healthy Living Unit
Jeanne Mance Building, 7th Floor
A.L. 1907C1
Tunney's Pasture
Ottawa, ON K1A 0K9
Canada
(613) 941-3109
Web site: http://www.phac-aspc.gc.ca/pau-uap/paguide/
   child_youth/index.html
   The Web site for Canada's Physical Activity Guides for
   Children and Youth provides links to relevant Internet
   resources.

Canadian Center on Substance Abuse
75 Albert Street, Suite 300
Ottawa, ON K1P 5E7
Canada

(613) 235-4048

Web site: http://www.ccsa.ca

The center was established to "mobilize collaborative efforts to reduce alcohol- and other drug-related harms."

Franklin Institute

222 North Twentieth Street

Philadelphia, PA 19103

(215) 448-1200

Web site: http://www.fi.edu

Founded in 1824, this scientific institute offers resources in many areas of science, health, and other topics.

Mayo Clinic

200 First Street SW

Rochester, MN 55905

(507) 284-2511

Web site: http://www.mayoclinic.com

The Mayo Clinic is a "not-for-profit medical practice dedicated to the diagnosis and treatment of virtually every type of complex illness."

National Institute of Mental Health

U.S. Department of Health and Human Services

6001 Executive Boulevard, Room 8184, MSC 9663

Bethesda, MD 20892-9663

(301) 443-4513, (866) 615-6464

Web site: http://www.nimh.nih.gov

This federal government organization is dedicated to the understanding and treatment of mental illnesses.

National Institute on Drug Abuse
National Institutes of Health
U.S. Department of Health and Human Services
6001 Executive Boulevard, Room 5213
Rockville, MD 20892-9561
(301) 443-1124
Web site: http://www.nida.nih.gov
 The institute seeks to bring "the power of science to bear on drug abuse and addiction."

Web Sites

Due to the changing nature of Internet links, Rosen Publishing has developed an online list of Web sites related to the subject of this book. This site is updated regularly. Please use this link to access this list:

http://www.rosenlinks.com/faq/sched

Bickerstaff, Linda. *Stress* (Coping in a Changing World). New York, NY: Rosen Publishing, 2007.

Engle, Janet. *101 Ways to Make Studying Easier and Faster for High School Students: What Every Student Needs to Know Explained Simply*. Ocala, FL: Atlantic Publishing, 2008.

Fox, Annie. *Too Stressed to Think? A Teen Guide to Staying Sane When Life Makes You Crazy*. Minneapolis, MN: Free Spirit Publishing, 2005.

Harmon, Daniel E. *Hallucinogens: The Dangers of Distorted Reality* (Drug Abuse and Society). New York, NY: Rosen Publishing, 2009.

Hipp, Earl. *Fighting Invisible Tigers: A Stress Management Guide for Teens*. 3rd ed. Minneapolis, MN: Free Spirit Publishing, 2008.

Hyde, Margaret O., and Elizabeth H. Forsyth. *Stress 101: An Overview for Teens*. Minneapolis, MN: Twenty-First Century Books, 2008.

Hyde, Margaret O., and John F. Setaro. *Drugs 101: An Overview for Teens*. Minneapolis, MN: Twenty-First Century Books, 2003.

Kirberger, Jesse, and Kimberly Kirberger. *I Don't Know What I Want But I Want to Be Happy*. Deerfield Beach, FL: Health Communications, Inc., 2009.

Mangrum, Charles T., II, and Stephen S. Strichart. *Study Skills and Strategies for Students in High School*. 2nd ed. Loveland, CO: Mangrum-Strichart Learning Resources, 2007.

Morgenstern, Julie, and Jessi Morgenstern-Colon. *Organizing from the Inside Out for Teenagers: The Foolproof System for Organizing Your Room, Your Time, and Your Life*. New York, NY: Henry Holt and Company, 2002.

Seaward, Brian, and Linda Bartlett. *Hot Stones and Funny Bones: Teens Helping Teens Cope with Stress and Anger*. Deerfield Beach, FL: Health Communications, Inc., 2002.

Verdick, Elizabeth, and Marjorie Lisovskis. *How to Take the GRRRR Out of Anger*. Minneapolis, MN: Free Spirit Publishing, 2003.

Index

About the Author

Daniel E. Harmon is the author of numerous books and magazine and newspaper articles. His books for adolescents and young adults include volumes on manic depression, schizophrenia, anorexia nervosa, and other psychological problems. *First Job Smarts* (Get Smart with Your Money) was published by Rosen in 2009, as was *Hallucinogens: The Dangers of Distorted Reality* (Drug Abuse and Society). He lives in Spartanburg, South Carolina.

Photo Credits

Cover © www.istockphoto.com; p. 5 © www.istockphoto.com/Petro Feketa; p. 7 © Sidney Moulds/Photo Researchers; pp. 8, 25 © Shutterstock; p. 11 © www.istockphoto.com/Daniel Bendjy; p. 15 © www.istockphoto.com/Jim Kolaczko; p. 17 © Jeff Greenberg/Photo Edit; p. 20 © David Young-Wolff/Photo Edit; p. 22 © www.istockphoto.com/Elana Korenbaum, p. 28 © www.istockphoto.com/James Boulette; p. 31 © www.istockphoto.com/Lisa F. Young; p. 34 © Sheila Terry/Photo Researchers; p. 37 © www.istockphoto.com/Igor Dutina; p. 39 © www.istockphoto.com/Frederick Kaselow; p. 44 © www.istockphoto.com/Joseph Abbott; p. 46 © Andersen Ross/Getty Images; p. 48 © Bonnie Kamin/Photo Edit; p. 50 © www.istockphoto.com/Nikola Hristovski; p. 52 © www.istockphoto.com/Alex Gumerov.

Designer: Nicole Russo; Editor: Kathy Kuhtz Campbell; Photo Researcher: Marty Levick